Awake to Clarity

Joseph Raffa

Awake to Clarity

Author: Joseph Raffa

Editor: Teena Raffa-Mulligan

ISBN: 978-0-9944990-5-9

eISBN: 978-0-9944990-8-0

Author's note: The term 'mankind' is used throughout this discourse in reference to the human race collectively.

Published by Sea Song Publications

sea-song@bigpond.com

www.seasongpublications.com

.1.

WE HAVE BEEN given many ways to draw us back to our Universal Source. Many enlightened ones have appeared among us to encourage our return. Still we wander, lost in the mists of time. We live in a no-man's land of non-discovery. We wither on the vine of life, listless and lifeless, ignoring the sustenance that is our life blood. Enclosed in a cocoon of isolation we languish, beset by all kinds of difficulties. We worship the ego, the littleness that appears on the surface, tend it with care and live in ignorance of "*That*" which is the Greater Self we belong to.

The world of appearance is paramount. What we see, touch, feel and taste, the sounds of creation dominate us. We live a dream and take this to be the only reality. The reflection is considered more important than "*That*" which casts the reflection. We are such a mixed up lot that we have a great deal of trouble trying to disentangle ourselves from our confusion. We go this way and that, listen to experts, cull the mind for worthwhile reasons and try different therapies. Yet still we are not light-hearted and free flowing in our approach and love is mostly absent in our relationships.

Understanding the self as it unfolds presents enormous difficulties. Here we are, in a position to observe what we are and do yet we are a major mystery to ourselves. We do not know what is going on in our bodies, in the deeper reaches of our nature, what motivates us to think, feel and act as we do. We confine ourselves to a surface and separate view and thereby limit our perceptions to what this is capable of knowing.

Along come mystics, enlightened ones overflowing with love for mankind, speaking a language that does not make much sense to the rational mind. They tell of a wondrous Silence that is beyond the mind, of the freedom and love that unfolds with its discovery. The heart pulls towards what they offer but the mind pulls away, back to its familiar place in time and its ever-changing panorama.

This life is so fascinating. There is so much that attracts us: the unfolding vista of nature, companionships and the creative outpouring of the mind in so many directions. Here we know ourselves, or think we do, and feel comfortable amidst our own kind. The Strangeness we hear tell of beyond time dances out of reach beyond our ken — so elusive, yet its call torments the heart and raises longings we do not understand. Through the mind we urge towards time, to all that we know. But we are more than the body that moves or the thoughts and feelings that ebb and flow. In the depths of what we are we share a strange nature.

This is what the mystics, those who are fully awake, draw attention to. They have penetrated past the outer covering humans wear and they dwell in this, the timeless nature that is everywhere present. They talk of this wonder, of the incapacity of thought to formulate it and present it in a reasonable manner so that others may come to know of it. The rational mind shrinks from this kind of talk. It cannot move where thinking is non-existent. It revels in the expression of thought, in apprehending the known. It pulls towards substance.

What else can it do? This is its business, to appreciate the world of thing-time. Yet could it but cease its idle chatter for a moment it could learn something of tremendous importance. In silence, when thought and sensation are absent, the self is not aware of itself in its usual camouflage of appearance. When self-existence fades, Universal Existence takes over — it is everywhere, thought free and immersed in its own nature.

One moment of realisation is all it takes to sweep doubts aside. Conviction comes with discovery. Not that the mind yields with just one moment of baptism but at least this is a beginning — the first input of truthful revelation and a retreat by false perception which formerly ruled undisturbed. This kind of truth is an incredible arising. It's so simple when it happens and so illuminating. It comes gift-wrapped in clear-view seeing. No digging and prying involved, no preparing the ground by logical reason. Just a surprise eruption.

Truth brings its own conviction. It has that kind of power. It cannot be manipulated for self-advantage. What is clearly seen is over. It can't be repeated. Inasmuch that the self is constantly undergoing change, so the truth must be ever fresh, ever new. To hark back to past insights to explain present situations is to lapse back into a false perspective. The self is only understood in the present. Miss the truth of the movement and it passes you by.

We have the capacity to understand anew from moment to moment. We fail to exercise it because the self intervenes with its own perspectives, its desire to protect and enhance itself, to adhere to its own adopted convictions, its own particular way of seeing things. To yield Self completely, to put it aside is a most arduous undertaking. It must be kept under surveillance unceasingly. Withdraw attention, even briefly, and it reasserts its intentions and its insistence to function according to its own inclinations. The self survives all kinds of hardships and setbacks, trials and tribulations and boomerangs back to maintain and expand its standing. It is the most stubborn movement in existence. Not the highest nature we are endowed with but the most persistent to continue in the grooves it is accustomed to.

It takes an overload of love and understanding, an input of divine grace to curtail its activity, to dissolve it so that it no longer acts as a barrier to living rightly. Whatever ideas and organisations it lives by, behind the frameworks and labels it adopts, it maintains its self-centred standing. And while it functions intact, established in its network and framework of ideas, traditions and usual standpoints as a self that is bent on more for itself, with self-preservation and expansion as its main theme, so true peace and harmony are absent.

A self that has not fully understood its own processes, that has not returned to its source in the Universal reflects a measure of disorder in its thinking, feelings and actions. This must be so even if it is not recognised as such or acknowledged by society. Order only flows from insight, understanding and love. It is not a straitjacket imposed by social legislation nor by individual decree. It is not bound by conditions nor manufactured by the mind. It makes its own way, a by-product of an awakened understanding, of a love that seeks no return. It cannot be artificially contrived by thought nor presented as an ideal to be lived up to.

Intelligence is its own solution to living. We are endowed with intelligence as a gift from Universal Life. It is the basis of our humanity. All nature's creatures reflect a measure of intelligence. The cosmos, all life reflects intelligent order. When our natural intelligence is not restricted by the ego bent on advancing its own causes, it functions beautifully to meet the needs of daily living. Intelligence is beyond the thinking ego's capacity to comprehend its nature. Its effects are observable and through this it demonstrates something of its nature.

We at least have the common sense to recognise that something unique is acting through us to project meaning and the understanding of what is taking place around and within us. We name this remarkable quality intelligence. It lifts us to the human level we display. To the degree we limit its function, we disadvantage ourselves and disarrange the social expression accordingly with wars, discord, starvation and want, racial and national prejudice and all else that is displeasing.

Likewise, to the degree we allow our innate intelligence to function without undue interference from the ego, so we reflect order and the more admirable qualities the human expression is capable of. Before intelligence can function as it should the nature of the ego and its role in the human expression must be thoroughly understood. Otherwise it behaves like a festering sore that never heals, nor does it reflect an inner healthy state and its behaviour becomes erratic and subject to the directives of fear, self-concern and greed for more. And this is no way for humans to live — fear ridden, wrapped in unproductive attitudes and influences that deny intelligence a clear outlet.

So we live using a fraction of our inner resources, being unbalanced in the sense that we are technologically efficient and going ahead like jets with a knowledge explosion that yet leaves the human race incapable of living joyously in peace and harmony, as an integrated unit functioning in time, blending together to reflect intelligence of a very high order.

Intelligence denied an outlet leaves the human race dismembered. Isolated centres, inward looking, are set up as expanded national, tribal and racial egos living behind physical and mental barriers. A vast enslavement of the human race through egoistic intention just to safeguard the established settlements of the ego, built up over centuries of ego dominance that has refused to yield to the higher directives of love and an intelligent appreciation of the living process.

Intelligence unrestricted sees the human race as one entity expressing itself in a variety of ways, yet essentially part of the One Universal Nature. Distinction is only on the surface and only of a minor consequence. What are language and physical differences, traditions and backgrounds but implanted tendencies, perhaps here today and gone tomorrow? The underlying Universal Nature inherent in all is enduring and consistent unto itself.

.2.

WE HAVE AN intellectual appreciation of life and this restricts the exploration of self and limits the functioning of intelligence. It restricts it to the level of thought. Like a train travelling on railway tracks is confined in its direction so too is intelligence when it relies solely on thought. It is limited to what thinking can produce and this is inevitably a thought-out conclusion that fits in with the level of intelligence that has not yet been liberated from egoistic control and allowed to run its own course.

This may seem a strange statement. Intelligence is not considered a quality other than under ego control. The ego is in a sense a malfunction, a centre that has broken away from the mainstream flow of life and pursues its own intentions. Instead of blending with the universal flow it sets itself up on an individual base and operates from there to preserve everything it has identified with. Self-interest as self-perceived comes first and foremost. Intelligence is bent in the service of the self, not allowed the freedom to expand from the narrow confines of serving the self and its gathering of personal interests.

Intelligence goes where it is directed — to act for and on behalf of the self, or it can set off on the greatest undertaking humans can be involved in: an exploration of the human content leading to union with the Universal Nature. An exploration controlled by the self is going nowhere. Acting from its individual base, from a limited understanding, it continues to cast shadows and problems and never deeply clarifies any aspect of its own behaviour. While it functions from its separatist standing it cannot see otherwise than from this narrow focus. It cannot approach and blend in with wholeness while fragmented. Experiencing wholeness heals the rifts caused by the surface self. The separatist process is necessary for surface living but it inhibits exploration of the deeper levels within the human expression. Intelligence needs to be free ranging to explore the deeper reaches of self-existence.

It's no good being chained to a surface viewpoint if you want to go deeper. If you stay on the surface then that's all you will observe — the usual familiar vista. Inner exploration is an entirely new journey. You do not know where you are going nor how to get there. The book of the inner self opens up its pages of its own accord and displays its contents for the unrestricted intelligence to absorb when the self has been put aside.

You cannot approach this with intelligence conditioned by knowledge and past experience, through the endeavours of a self that is riddled with the effects of time. That is the difficulty we face — to bypass everything we have accumulated, every self-consideration and manifestation. Hold to even a little of this and it will prevent realisation of what is obvious to true perception.

Self is clutter, Self obscures, Self is not Light. Though it preens itself on its acquired knowledge, facts and figures, its knowledge is shallow in depth, though vast in extent. It can build and it can destroy. Its dreams go up in the smoke of disruption. It travels everywhere but inwards, over land, sea, across space but not inwards towards the core of what it is. The human expression limits itself to the spark of self-consciousness, thence to an intellectual approach.

Everything is detailed out in thoughts. The language of the mind takes over. Self lives in the language, not in the reality of what is ongoing. Reality is total, not divided, whereas Self comes to the fore through distinction. Without separation and distinction there is no sense of self. The observing sensitivity draws apart from the flow of experience then perceives it as the outer and itself as localised within the body. Perception is distorted with localisation, when the self limits itself to what it appears to be, when it takes separation to be an absolute truth.

It is difficult to bypass the hypnotic effect of appearance and penetrate to the underlying reality, the One nature that pervades all. Effort, reflection by the self continues the charade of distinction. Separation will not be reasoned away. The effect is ingrained, going deep inwardly where the belief holds sway. The texture of human living is fashioned on separation. All the talk in the world, even the desire to experience reality will not shift it.

Self is convinced of the reality of individuality as indisputable. Every movement to affirm or deny merely confirms self-existence. What affirms, what denies: is this not the self that seeks the underlying nature of Oneness? The dominance of the intellect, this too confirms and strengthens separation. Wherever the self parades itself, in whatever mood or form, thought or feeling, the accent is on separation.

To bring an end to it, Self must simultaneously end too. Remove Self from the scene and separation dissolves. An act of will cannot do this. The actor with the intention is part of the self. The act of willing emanates from the self. That which calls itself 'self' has misunderstood its nature. It has accepted a mirage as factual, decreed itself to be limited in appearance and denied the reality of what it is in essence. It's in love with its own shadow, lives the life of the shadow, dresses this up in substance, in thoughts and sensations and keeps emphasising distinction.

Meanwhile the Light that casts the shadow is relegated to the backwoods, not acknowledged, not confirmed, its existence unknown. The Light of the universe, the One Light, the only Light is neglected while the shadow runs riot doing its own thing.

The spark that animates the shadow, that breathes being into it remains an enigma. The shadow cavorts in the limelight of timeful existence, delights in its bodily appearance, enjoys the pleasures of the senses, shrinks from pain, does its best to avoid the unpleasant and lets life go by with little concern for what makes it possible to be here. Its life ebbs and flows, swinging from one extreme to the other. Shadow self stumbles onwards, oscillating to and fro, from one emotion to another, drives this way then that with desire at the helm, or perhaps fear. Always seeking stability, psychological security, stimulation, whatever meets with its approval.

To observe it impartially as it goes about its business is a revelation in learning. This requires moments of detachment, of not being fully immersed in the self. Then it begins to reveal its hidden secrets, what it isn't aware of about its own nature. In these spontaneous moments of quiet watchfulness the self is observed as you would natural scenery — deeply absorbed without the distraction of thinking, without resistance.

The self cannot be understood in its totality if one takes only a surface view. This touches the outer aspects but leaves the inner side untouched. The self is a composite of its outer features and all that goes on inwardly. By no means a fixture easily kept under review, it is constantly shifting ground as it responds to stimuli and surrounding experience. For sure the outer appearance is well defined but it is not with this that any trouble usually lies. Rather it is in keeping up with the deeper levels of its nature, in understanding its interior workings.

The use of reason also needs refining as a learning instrument. Thought has the capacity to explain much but it's confined in its movement. It has difficulty in going beneath the surface to focus on what is happening there. Thinking is a distraction, an impediment to understanding the movement of the self. This requires total attention, undivided attention in which the observer unifies with the observed. The distinction, the apparent gap felt to be real and actual between the observing sensitivity and that which is under observation drops away. Only the observing element prevails. Without this nothing could be known or experienced. This is paramount, primary. All else is secondary no matter how dominant it appears when apprehended through the senses.

What appears to the observer draws the greater emphasis to itself. The impact of the known is so powerful. This cannot be ignored. Self-attention is therefore outward bound, to the known world and the care of the self. The inner side, not being obvious to the senses or in some way recognised by the observing self, is ignored, even denied and not considered worthy of the same attention relegated to the outer aspects of the self and its environment. In the world of time, the march of the mind takes over and becomes an avalanche of thoughts, intentions, explanations, desires and directives, all intended to serve the self. All drifting, dancing, energetically driving along to objective after objective. That is how the self keeps itself going. Action is its theme song, not stillness. So it misses out on the joy, on the return that deep stillness brings when it happens. It does not realise the depth of its loss.

Here it is with a treasure trove of value it has yet to realise. It dances in the limelight of consciousness where the self is king and queen and action is the thing that counts. Until old age slows it down and death carts it away. So it goes from birth to death without realising its true nature. Rarely does it investigate its own content with the intention of delving to the very depths of its being. It does not discard the debris accumulated through timeful living — all the covering overlay of memories, sensations, the outer structure it knows so well and the inner movement of thought and feeling. All this masks the underlying purity, the nature that thought cannot embrace, the essence that flows into appearance to manifest as the self and its surroundings.

Self is a tangle of contradictions, a complex expression of many interacting strands. Simplicity is not the keynote of its endeavours. Its approach to life is through the mind. Techniques, programs, methods are the mind's forte. The longer the mind continues in time its approach becomes more technical, more complex. The result is knowledge, an accumulation of experience, facts, the result of generations of investigation and applied endeavour in diverse directions.

So the expert mind is born, settles in and is lifted onto a pedestal of importance, to be consulted in all matters of consequence. To be expert requires study, tests, exams, university courses. Those who pass advertise themselves and become prominent members of the social community, addressed in time of need.

.3.

WITH THE GROWING awareness of the need for change, for improvement in health and wellbeing, new experts have come to the fore. This is the era of the New Age movement, with its own culture, literature, various offerings in self-improvement with confident advertisements stating what New Age experts can help you do. They offer health, wealth, inner balance, spiritual awareness, control of the mind. Now the self has new avenues to expand into, to support it in its quest for greater self-expression. More methods, more techniques to be involved in. Benefits there may well be but a self in constant movement, always flowing towards desired results is difficult to pin down, to coax into stillness, the kind that is not induced by self-intention, by mind manipulation.

Whatever emanates from the self is a limited projection and never transcends this boundary. Try as it may, the self can never through its own efforts break out of the barriers that are a consequence of its own endeavours. All it can do is acknowledge that they are there, that they rise because of its limited understanding about its own processes. Otherwise, if its understanding was flawless, the barriers would not be there and the self would be living in the light of a clear understanding.

Self in its movement casts an array of concepts, ideas and beliefs. These it holds to as factual until reason decrees otherwise. The array is extensive, expanding year by year. New additions replace the old, whatever is considered obsolete. There is a grand parade in time, the self in search of a wider truth, improved living, sorting out difficulties, individual, national, international — a steady progress that sometimes proceeds with little interruption. But more often there are snags and troubles due to the self's inability to harmonise with itself, others and surroundings.

The planet reverberates with the concerted sounds of the self in action. A torrent of energy, thought and feeling pouring into time, forming separate strands; whirlpools breaking away from the main flow of life and settling into organised backwaters, like characteristics drawing unto like characteristics. National, religious and social movements, strand on strand; the old adapting, changing, new strands appearing, gaining adherents as people are stirred by desire into a ferment of change; into a constant search for the new, for better than what they have.

Self is the overseer, the evaluator and decision maker. What it wants, what it sees value in are the deciding factors in where it goes from here. Desires intermixed, perhaps a sprinkling of fear, demands and needs all interacting to influence the self in its constant journey for self- improvement. A burgeoning tide always on the move, day by day. Night brings a brief respite but with the coming of the day, so the drive of the self arises anew to continue its customary journey through life.

Each individual is a part of something bigger, a small social cog in the state and national organisation. The state, the nation is an extension of the self, magnified by addition of like-minded and thinking people. They adhere together with the glue of common ideas, of traditional ways and even through fear, the need for protection from aggression. These are the basic foundations on which are laid the variable expressions extant worldwide.

As long as these foundations hold firm, the organisational self, the state and national self maintains its identity. The operating influences go deep indeed. Although it appears these are willingly accepted and allowed to dictate the course and direction the self undertakes in life, the continuity of social, state and national characteristics are maintained by the conditioning by association that takes place from childhood. The exposure is such that outer conditions infiltrate to mould thoughts and feelings in favour of, or acceptance of the surrounding social mores.

This is an extensive and prolonged association deliberately or unconsciously encouraged by adults, education systems and government agencies. The sensitive human material is moulded from an early age and so the self becomes imprisoned in an enclosure of influences, attitudes, traditions and outlooks that are considered an expression of free choice rather than an authoritative implant. The result is considered to be the best by far of a long line of social adaptation.

The result is that the original human material has a lesser self, a shadow imposed that takes over to control the human expression and its direction of travel. The shadow thinks, feels and speaks for the whole person. The inner person remains a mystery unto itself while the shadow basks in the limelight of importance and carries on seemingly independent and in full and free charge of all it does. Yet in effect it is socially enslaved and bound by restrictions that insist it is a distinctive individual, nationally, socially, religiously, by the social characteristics that predominantly shape it.

The pages of a new life are relatively free of social imprint early on. As the self expands in its awareness of its surroundings, so this changes. The pages begin to fill with the social register and this becomes the background from which the self acts and refers to as it develops. Gradually humans are moulded into a particular kind of social expression. Originality is blocked and the shadow imposition predominates to spread a shade of darkness over the social landscape. Beneath this overlay lies the purity that is the essential nature of the self. Before the imprint of time takes over, this essence alone is. While the imprint is ongoing this underlying nature remains uncontaminated, untouched and inviolate.

In dealing with the aspirations and complex movement of the self, concepts are created as a means of expression and to convey meaning to others. They are shaped by thought out of its capacity to create meaning of a particular kind, a language of sorts that the self has in common with others. The transmission of concepts is an essential aspect of self-existence. They are extremely flexible and cover a wide range of matters dealt with by the self. They cannot convey reality, only concepts.

Everything the self touches via thought is limited in range by its depth of understanding and by the nature of thought to grasp only the kind of meaning and images it can deal with. And this surely is not the totality of life which includes all levels of intelligence, below and above man's as it now operates, and complex universal systems that are yet to be fully understood.

Reality is often discussed and sought for. How the mind can pursue this without having any experience of what it is, whether it exists and how it relates to the phenomenal world is somewhat of an enigma. Ideas, theories, its own projections, these are familiar ground to the thinking intellect. Perhaps this is what the self aims for, a reality fabricated by itself. Otherwise why does it involve itself in methods and techniques that are supposedly avenues towards the promised land of Ultimate Reality? In any case, in its search for truth, reality, or its idea of Heaven, Self withdraws itself from what it is searching for, considers itself separate from the projected objectives, then works like a beaver to reach the unknown goal.

Take note of the word *unknown* because before any realisation takes place, Ultimate Reality and deeper truths about the self's nature are precisely that. Yet, the self ventures forth hell-bent on discovery for what lies beyond its ken, confident that through effort applied from misunderstanding, worthwhile discovery will follow. Persistent travel from its limited resources and the lack of worthwhile returns for effort expended eventually sinks in. The result? The perceptive self comes to a standstill, having reached the end of the line known as self-effort.

If the letting go that follows is spontaneous and total then the stage is set for a revelatory input. As the self fades out of the picture as a struggling, striving entity, what is everywhere present comes into view. This happening clears away confusion and clear-view seeing takes over. The subject/object relationship is momentarily dropped. Self is the basis of this apparent division and with its temporary demise, so it disappears. The trouble is, thinking too ends with the self. It doesn't carry on to grasp what happens so the existence of the Universal, although now confirmed by discovery, is unexplainable in reasonable terms. There is a selfless, choiceless awareness that records and the certitude filters down to the self when it returns to its accustomed role in timeland.

Obviously then, what considers itself to be the self, that limits itself to a separate individual role, does so only in appearance and not as an undeniable fact of life. For if the division from the Universal nature was irrevocably so, *"That"* which masqueraded as the self in time could not be drawn back into and realise this surprising truth when the self ceased to function in its usual role. Only through realisation, through experiencing the state when Self is absent does this become clear and in no other way. Otherwise, what we are is locked into its world of space, time and customary experience and doesn't break out of this time-bound prison to merge with what lies beyond.

So life, through integration, reveals its deepest secret and a new approach begins to operate. Self begins to recede as the most significant side of the human expression. It has a resiliency to keep bouncing back into the limelight and holding on. Its separate role is deeply ingrained. But *"That"* which reveals its nature in the moments of self-absence persuades without intention or power, just by virtue of being what it is, by the truth and the insightful understanding that follows.

What could be better? To be clear like crystal water, free flowing, unhindered by the self's particular idiosyncrasies. This is surely something to reach out for, to realise and to move with —or do we remain in the shadow self with its frustrations, heartaches, its constant obsession to establish itself through desire and achievement? Self wants to remain embedded in timeful endeavour. This is reassuring to the self. It is a life it is comfortable with.

However there is a side to life that is painful and troublesome when lived in this way. The potential for suffering follows the self wherever it goes, whatever it does. There is no escape, no easy ride for the self that lives on the outer edge of life, in the shadows, wrapped in a surface contemplation that does not deeply investigate its own movement. Too many influences urge it this way and that. Fear, desires, demands, concerns, ambitions and greed contend for control. At the helm is the self that sits in judgment and relies on choice to decide what is acceptable, pleasant and worthwhile and what will be resisted and rejected.

Who is eager to row the boat of investigation into the dark and stormy sea of the self? With so much that is pleasurable to reach out for and that promises much in self-satisfaction and sensual enjoyment, who will turn away and devote time and attention to investigating the inner and outer aspects of the self? It is so much easier to roll along with the tide of usual self-involvement with life than to undertake a rigorous inquiry into what is going on.

Self is only interested in foreseeable returns, not in possible revelations that may or may not arise. It does not know of any profitable return that insights into self-behaviour may bring. So it prefers the direction of travel that it knows rather than stir itself to move in a direction that requires total commitment and full attention and looms as a vast unknown. Besides, it is usually quite content to continue as it is with a little adjustment here and there as the need arises. It considers that it is a bright light in the world and not in any need of a profound change in understanding or in any way that it behaves or how it sees things.

.4.

LIFE HAS ITS own way of calling out to humans, of stirring them inwardly to change tack, and redirecting the attention from outer affairs to the inner level of thoughts, feelings, attitudes and mental reactions. The inner is a hive of activity spilling its consequences into the outer. What predominates inwardly determines the outer face of the self. Seeing this is so, rather than modifying the self with a touch of discipline here and there, directed by the self, isn't it better to observe with deep attention what goes on, what the self gives out in response to the outer flow of experience? In this there is the opportunity to develop understanding of the right kind and this effects a release from the limited confines of the self.

So often we impose and superimpose beliefs, modifying aspects of the self that please and satisfy through indulgence and discipline, giving the impression that one is advancing and improving. These kinds of benefits are somewhat brittle, not deep rooted because they are not founded on the firm base of a deep understanding of what is involved. A lapse of attention and they are swept away even if entrenched through habitual application. What the self insists on doing, what the more powerful desires and demands are, will break out when the covering veneers of disciplinary control slip a little.

Right understanding does not arise from the partial and limited standing often displayed by the self. It arises from a wider and deeper perception, from a level that embraces the self and its surroundings in a unity without any distinction whatsoever. This is not brought about by conscious endeavour, nor is it a result of unconscious endeavour but rises from above and beyond the self as we know it. It flows in to infuse the self — a gift of grace that dispels the gloom, doom and darkness of the self by illumination and revelation. Its coming shatters the conditioned, age-old hold of the self and its narrow, selective way of looking at everything.

Self, in the course of its movement, through social contact and individual acceptance has collected an overburden of erroneous perceptions and accepted attitudes fashioned by an influx of influences. A modifying agency is at work, filtering and screening experience and the incoming material, accepting or rejecting according to self-determination. This becomes the base for the expression of the self at work, at play in whatever the self undertakes to do.

To get down to bedrock, to see what the true nature of the self is before this overlay gets in the way and takes over, this overburden has to be shifted, shoved out completely. Otherwise it will contaminate any investigation and control the movement towards truthful discovery and nullify an impartial approach. Any residue of this contamination will influence and dictate to some degree not only the course of the investigation but also the conclusions arrived at and accepted. How then is a self that is trapped in this residue to extricate itself and bypass this morass of accumulated beliefs, attitudes and acquired information gathered by the self and held in its memory banks, ever ready to be drawn on as the occasion arises?

Beneath this overlay lies the purity of our essential nature. Yet any movement that springs from the background inevitably keeps the focus of attention locked into this background. It only produces what the background is capable of — that is, more of the same — thoughts, feelings, techniques and methods that keep the self locked into effort and practice, into the usual sense of separation, of being individually contained. This in no way shatters this psychological prison to allow the essence of "*What Is*" to experience its own nature just as it is.

As long as the self has faith in its background to produce worthwhile results it will keep adding new material to it and continue to rely on it for support, inspiration and guidance in the business of living. This serves well enough for much that we do in those aspects where experience, memory and knowledge are necessary. This is acknowledged but it fails dismally to carry us forward into a clear understanding of the self and its inner workings. It does not make truthful revelation possible, nor does it bring an end to all the dark and dreary facets expressed when the self sleeps on in its ignorance and has not breached the barriers that prevent realisation of its true nature.

A big difficulty in opening up to self-understanding lies in the fact that the self insists on being a dominant part of the show, shaping the procedures put into operation. Its experience of life is that worthwhile results accrue only through involvement, effort and application. One can't deny that lack of interest and inattention lead nowhere of value. These then are prerequisites for learning.

But if the self that is responsible for social troubles, for expressing disruption and all else that leads to disharmony continues to act from the same base without first discarding through enlightened understanding the self-centred thinking that generates disharmony, then it remains in the same confines. The social barometer will not swing to sunshine but remains fixed on inclement human behaviour.

.5.

HUMAN NATURE HAS been stuck in the doldrums of social disturbance for thousands of years. No vast stirring to lead mankind into enduring peace and plentiful enjoyment has yet produced this kind of harvest. We've had some outstanding persons drop in now and again who demonstrated what could be accomplished by tapping into Universal resources — by putting aside the personal self and realising *"That"* nature that is its essential reality.

So began the great religions. These served as a means for further divisions, more violence and set the scene for disagreement and disputation by followers who failed to get past the written word to the underlying meaning offered. Yet those inspired advocates of enlightened living brought something priceless to their fellow humans and demonstrated its value in their personal lives in the way they lived it. They could hardly be blamed that so few rose to the occasion, realised the meaning behind the words and in their turn became centres of a new and inspired expression.

Nowadays the word has spread far and wide. New variations of what is essentially the same message are flowing out into the social marketplace challenging the role of the older religions. What appealed in the past does not have the same impact today. Although its value is acknowledged, what has developed around the original fresh and inspired offerings — the organisations and authority, the rigid insistence to adhere to age-old traditions, the constant repetition of the written word — this has turned sensitive people elsewhere in a search for encouragement, for something they can relate to that satisfies the inner urge to find deeper meaning and value in a life that reflects so much that is displeasing.

People will not remain satisfied with the written word, with explanations and reasons forever no matter how convincing they sound. In matters spiritual they will insist on realisation, on experiencing not only the truth of what is ongoing in their lives but more importantly that nature referred to as the Essence, the Universal, the Oneness or God. Feeding on words is lean food indeed. There is no deep nourishment in this. It serves as an aperitif, an introduction to the main spiritual course. Momentary interludes in which the self is absent in its familiar role as an individual and the divine takes over in its totality is what nourishes, revitalises and renews the human spirit. Without experiencing Oneness the human expression is locked into separation, division and distinction. The surface self becomes entrenched on this level and ignorance of its true nature takes over when the discovery of Oneness is unrealised.

Oneness as a reality confounds the mind. It is much more comfortable amongst the many. Indeed this is its function, to acknowledge and deal with the many. The mind of the many does not experience the

One. What then does? Only that which is the same in essence. This bars thought, feelings, sensations, even the observer that acknowledges distinction, a sense of being apart from that which is experienced. Much of what is recognised as the self is a breakaway movement from the universal background and forms a conscious expression by which it is recognised and known. The mind of the many comes into its own on this level. It becomes conditioned on this level by the flow of experience, the nature of space and time and by its own lack of true perception as to the ongoing true nature of reality.

The many mind is complex. It feeds on words, thoughts, explanations, reasons — the more the merrier. These are its lifeblood, coursing through the mind, filling it with ideas, images, concepts, initiating actions, creating beliefs and theories. Extensive indeed are the projections of the mind. They range far and wide covering the human expression, the universe, space and time, the past, the depth of nature's expression with a concourse of thoughts.

This outer activity takes over and becomes the be-all of the mind's approach. What cannot be conveyed by reason doesn't count. What isn't observed, that doesn't register in some way lacks evidential status. The many mind remains anchored in the known. And the known is sensations — sounds, sights, colours, forms — sense-based phenomena, seemingly fixed, solid and substantial but in actuality fleeting impressions arising from moment to moment and blended together by the mind's retentive capacity into having continuous extent in time. So we live out our dream, such as it is, fascinated by the outer movement, and ignore the miraculous inner reality, the amazing nature that is its source.

.6.

ON THE ONE hand we are creatures of flesh and blood, thought and feeling, our environment solid and spacious in appearance. This is the observed. We have an unobserved side, untouched by thought, feeling or time, the mystical side if you like — the untouchable, the incorruptible, unbridgeable by thought. Yet it may be realised and yield evidence of its nature in moments free of the known. In these, the subject/object relationship vanishes. Yet we are not annihilated.

What fades into the mysterious silence of the Ultimate Reality re-emerges in the accustomed manner. Life continues as usual. But the understanding changes. It deepens, the deception the self is caught up in is beginning to be exposed. This was hidden before, so well camouflaged by self-justification and supported by reason that it became deeply entrenched and acceptable to the self as the norm without question or challenge. Through the desire to support itself, its background and standing, the self weaves a web of subtle intrigue. It defends its established domain with might and main. All its defensive armoury is brought to bear if it feels itself and its kind threatened in any way. Possessions, connections, extensions, relationships, its adopted standpoints on a range of issues, its way of life, what it is drawn to — all this, the self's private domain and its outer ramifications, it will move to protect. This is hallowed ground to the self, the basis for its existence, its background meaning for living.

Self acts from a collective, a gathering of influences, attitudes and ideas, a memory content focused in the present via the physical body. Identification brings it all together. The over-riding thought — the "*I*", the "*me*" — is the link that gives it focus, purpose and meaning. An amazing process is abroad, complex yet compact, diverse yet woven together and functioning in a purposeful manner. It has a surface side, observable, identifiable and coherent in its function. Much of it operates outside conscious awareness and still fits in with the movement of the self, is indeed an integral part of its existence. Self is a much wider being than it knows. Not till the deeper aspects reveal their nature does the self acknowledge this. Otherwise, it has no direct evidence and so continues to live entrenched in its outer appearance and depend on thought to make matters clear.

Awareness yields the self verification of what it knows. What comes into its field of awareness and registers there is granted some measure of reality. Experience must impact on the self and draw attention to itself to stir recognition of its existence. In fact, whatever exists does so because of the primary nature of awareness. Awareness is taken for granted in the business of knowing. Brain is given paramount importance and is considered the source of consciousness — being aware. Yet awareness refuses to be pinned down as a factor in its own right.

What then do words relate to? How do they come to be in use in everyday language without clear evidence of what they stand for? It is like the word *mind* we use so freely as if it's an old friend. There is no argument about thoughts, feeling, body, brain, for of these things we have observational evidence. How then do we prove the existence of the nature of awareness, mind, consciousness apart from inference? With consciousness we may say being active, awake, fully functional in comparison to being unconscious due to whatever cause.

The light of a strange sensitivity is ongoing in us. It is not discernible objectively yet still it lights up experience and living in a meaningful way so that we know we are here and what is going on around us. Ideas proliferate in the self. They form and reform, adapt and change. They expand in all directions. What isn't experienced directly or known clearly is often the basis of a vigorous arising of ideas. They are used to define the nature of life, God, the universe. It's often ideas first then the backup of facts. If this isn't forthcoming to satisfaction then ideas are discarded or modified until ideas and facts merge in a unified expression considered to be truth as validated by observation and reasonable reflection.

The process of thinking, (the basis of ideas), is ever busy leading an investigative assault on all aspects of phenomenal appearance, life forms, the Earth and beyond, the human body, its functions and afflictions. After centuries of incessant use it has been honed to an intensity and reflective sharpness that puts it in the forefront of human endeavour. What is not worth thinking about is not considered significant. What is detailed and expressed in complex systems of thought is considered of great erudition, value and the acme of human intelligence.

"Think" was the urging of our teachers in our schooldays as they encouraged us on to higher achievements in learning. So we settled into thinking as the means to advance through life, to make decisions, to clear the way past, over or through obstacles. Thinking ranges everywhere, reaching its most intricate expressions in science, philosophy, religion and politics.

What then reflects its nature as thought, feeling, that manifests consciously in a variety of expressions yet still maintains a sense of unified purpose and functions as a self? It interlinks with a body, with the surrounding environment and develops relationships and above all gives rise to a flow of words and explanations, forging a language of explicit meaning that spreads out to cover all it comes into contact with. Almost instinctively every question is fashioned in words and answered in like manner.

One could well say that humans are a process of thinking, constantly in motion, expressed inwardly and outwardly in verbal parlance. So much so that thought predominates, taking over as the medium of understanding and communication. Yet the thought process is only part of the gateway to understanding. More important is the sensitivity that sets thought into motion and translates it into instant meaning. This is the core nature of what humans are. It is not confined to thoughts and sensations, is not observable nor fixed in substance. Yet it lights up the observed world, not only into being known but also imparts sense and coherency so that humans can function intelligently throughout their lifetimes.

.7.

TOTAL RELIANCE ON thinking as the way to go limits the self to what thinking can produce. It is remarkably effective to a degree, producing results that are everywhere evident. In the fields of organisation, the investigation of natural phenomena, laying out social guidelines, pushing the frontiers of knowledge ever outwards, its achievements are considerable. But humans will never reach their full potential via the thinking process alone.

The expressions of joy, of gentle living, of not giving out the dark side in human nature, the love of fellowman, are not the result of applied thinking. Thinking can organise to repair damage caused by warfare, by nature's violent upheavals, minimise sickness and alleviate pain but it cannot guarantee that humans will sparkle with goodness and live in wisdom and understanding as a consequence. It cannot take humans into the inner depths of what they are. It can discuss, theorise, reflect, consider options, present alternatives, ideas and concepts but the reality of what we are is beyond its grasp.

The grandness of life is not a thought-created concept. It must be observed directly without thoughts intervening offering explanations, translations and interpretations that are merely offshoots of a surface understanding that has never shifted from a self-centred and isolated standing. To observe directly is not to perceive from the surface level of the self acting from a separatist stance. Nor is it to rely on thinking to come to thought-created conclusions.

It is not fashioned by thought. It is spontaneous and arises when the self and its ramifications of thought, feeling and sensation come to a natural standstill. With nothing to interfere, direct observation happens. There is neither an observer nor the observed. A shift away from the known has taken over. Goodbye self in its usual role for a moment. Hello to the universal, to "*That*" which always is and never is not.

Regardless of what is going on in time this nature remains consistent unto itself. Change proceeds on the surface, the universal is untouched by it. So we go from sound to silence, from the seen to the unseen, from the many to the One, from separation to unity, from distinction to the undifferentiated. What do these words mean? Not the meaning that the self gives through the measure of understanding it has of words. The meaning comes through only when it happens, when the self and everything it is involved with drops away for a moment and instantaneously the universal is revealed. Call it what you like — enlightenment, revelatory insight, a spiritual breakthrough, a sudden awakening. The words do not matter, only the happening does. And when it does, it cannot be conveyed to another via the usual channels of communication so that another comes into it by word alone.

One offers the bait of reasonable involvement to whoever may be inwardly ready to accept it. What they do with it, how they respond is their business and becomes their journey. Should they wander unproductive avenues in their search for the Golden Strangeness (my name for the universal nature), that too is part of their learning. As realisation dawns, so they will discard what proves to be false and merely self-delusion and renew the search for that which is enduringly real.

Every springboard, whatever it be that the self launches itself from, is bound to exhaust itself fruitlessly in the field of time. It begins from here, remains here while effort continues and while it persists and never breaks through the barriers that lock the self into time. And being locked into time there is no going beyond to "*That*" which is beyond all time and space frames of reference. Not that travel is involved, it is just a sudden switch from the familiar world we know to the underlying reality, the One we do not know until realisation takes place via the experiencing of it.

With this sudden awakening a new learning is ushered in, one that cannot be learnt via text books or the spoken word. These offer encouragement to apply one's self and take those who are interested as far as the written and spoken word can do so. Then the individual is left to go on from there to explore the inner reaches of the self, to go where it has not gone before, to move into the formerly inaccessible territory of the unconscious and then beyond that till it lodges in the unknown nature of the Spiritual Strangeness.

To follow this through the use of reason alone is to bog down in the intricate projections that thought is capable of. Thinking will stretch every which way to reassure itself that it is on the right track, even convince itself that it understands what is involved just by listening to the "word". But life itself is not a word, not a thought; nor is the self a collection of explanations carefully framed. What life is, what the self is must be experienced from moment to moment, not only the surface aspects which are so paramount and observable but also the inner which not only proceeds with the outer but is also integrated with it.

To deeply understand the human expression throughout its nature one must leave the level of thought where it belongs and where it is of service — on the outer edge of life. Attention must focus below the surface or else it will fail to realise what is unfolding within. The remarkable inner world will remain an enigma, something to think about, to imagine and to speculate about but the truth of it will pass on by. Reflective thought always wants to move ahead and pave the way.

A thought-created roadway is fashioned and laid out for the self to move along. Self wanders from thought to thought-created avenues. Rarely does it leave the safety, the comfort, the familiarity of thought-created effort — the pathways, the choices, the initiatives fashioned by reason. So, one thoughtful step plods after the other on thought-created ground towards a thought-devised objective. The intention?

Protection, profit and pleasure for the self with comfort and a minimum of displeasing disturbance as parallel considerations.

Remain in the extensions of the self and you will never reach the promised land of spiritual discovery. Nor shall you break out of the confines the self has enclosed itself in. These confines are not acknowledged by the self. They are accepted as its normal life patterns, even as what it chooses to do. It sees no need to challenge its own establishment, to stir and dig its own content out from its hidden corners and flush the contamination out into the light of an honest and impartial appraisal. So much of this content is hidden from conscious sight.

Only an awareness that can range swiftly from the outer to the inner can expose what is ongoing in the inner reaches. And it needs to be exposed if the self is to understand the influences that control its actions and behaviour. Not many have the desire or the interest to venture this way. The outer has many attractions, the inner is a hidden extent not easily accessible. Nor is the value of an inner awakening recognised whereas the value accorded the outer is readily acknowledged.

Outward bound then is the urgent drive of the self, into sensations, experience, into the delights and offerings of timeland. There is much to enjoy here and if pain and the like intrude occasionally, then so be it as long as pleasure predominates and desires are not unduly frustrated. But a higher calling keeps knocking on the door of life and the sensitive ones recognise its value and respond accordingly. They cannot resist the inner call.

They long to come to rest in the one true home. There is no map precisely marked out to show the way, but undeterred by difficulties raised by the mind bent on self-protection they brush aside the whispers of security from the established lifestyle and proceed to venture into the unknown. They are explorers of a different mould. They are leaving the past with its overlay of experience and accustomed ways. Not for them the traditional ground to walk upon, or the support of social trends and established national and religious structures in their search.

In their urge to travel lightly they divest themselves of all impediments that detract from self-discovery, that may hold them back to the reassuring world of the known and prevent the uncovering of the new. They are not interested in the old projected in a new guise. The end of the old — completely — and the advent of the new, this is what they hope to realise.

And in realising this they come to ground in the Spiritual Strangeness, the essence of what they are, and live accordingly what flows from this fusion with the Universal Nature.

About the author

JOSEPH RAFFA WAS born in 1927 in Fremantle, Western Australia. He enjoyed an idyllic childhood roaming the bush and the seashore. In his teens Joseph became a dedicated atheist, looking to science for answers to the riddles of life and the universe. Then, in his early twenties, he experienced a moment of discovery that transformed his life. As Joseph's life opened out spiritually following this awakening, he was inspired to put pen to paper to encourage others to embark on their own journey of discovery.

Joseph died of cancer in 2010, leaving behind a legacy of inspirational writing which is now being made available to a wider audience. Visit www.towardsthesilentheart.com for more information about Joseph and his books.

Other books by Joseph Raffa

Beside Still Waters

ISBN 9780987227676

This beautiful collection of essays touches on the universal search for meaning and inspires readers to reach out for the still waters of the spirit.

The human heart longs for peace and harmony. It seeks a restful haven from the relentless busyness of everyday life, drawing us to spend tranquil moments in natural surrounds that offer a brief respite from the hustle and bustle. There is a state of inner stillness, when the endless chatter of the mind has ceased, that a deeper understanding arises. These are the 'still waters' that bring new life to mankind, that lay claim to the heart and redirect the mind. These are the waters of peace, love and true togetherness that lift us up to divine heights of being and living.

The Silent Guardian

ISBN 9780987227669

A timely reminder of our spiritual journey and true purpose on Earth.

Joseph shares an inspirational message for those who care to listen.

Explore the planets, the outer reaches of space, the depths of the seas. Burrow into the earth, climb every mountain. When you have seen it all, you will still be left with the mystery of yourself. Turn and face this. Explore this. When you've travelled the extent and depth of the human expression, much of what you learn will be beyond the mind's capacity to convey through verbalisation. When heart speaks to heart, what more is there to say?

The Silent Guardian

Beyond the Cross

The Christ Collection

ISBN 9780987227652

A moving collection of inspired pieces about Jesus.

Joseph Raffa was a dedicated atheist when he set out in search of answers to the riddles of life and the universe. Then, in a blissful moment of discovery, the God the Bible speaks of, the Allah of Mohammed and the longed for Nirvana of the Buddhists came into his life. As his life opened out spiritually, Joseph began to have a deeper appreciation of Jesus, His life and His role in the spiritual awakening of Mankind. Visions and insights arose unbidden, in such a manner that their authenticity could not be questioned. The young man who was an atheist for a time, who cared not to read the Bible or take much notice of Christ and His life, found himself anchored in God and also writing pieces extolling the virtues, the wisdom and the love expressed by that super spiritual being of long ago.

Thank you for taking the time to read this book. Ratings and reviews are appreciated. If you enjoyed it, please Tweet/Share on your social media networks.

www.ingramcontent.com/pod-product-compliance
Lightning Source LLC
Chambersburg PA
CBHW060713030426
42337CB00017B/2856